Girls' Health™

Seeing the Gynecologist

Sophie Waters

rosen publishing's
rosen central®

New York

Published in 2008 by The Rosen Publishing Group, Inc.
29 East 21st Street, New York, NY 10010

First Edition

Library of Congress Cataloging-in-Publication Data

Waters, Sophie.
Seeing the gynecologist/Sophie Waters.
   p. cm.—(Girls' health)
Includes bibliographical references and index.
ISBN-13: 978-1-4042-1948-9
ISBN-10: 1-4042-1948-X
1. Teenage girls—Medical examinations—Juvenile literature. 2. Gynecology—
Juvenile literature. 3. Generative organs, Female—Juvenile literature.
I. Title.
RG122.W38 2007
618.1—dc22

                                                              2007001633

Manufactured in the United States of America

Contents

Introduction

If you are a teenager, chances are you have noticed changes in your body. Your figure may have become curvy. Your breasts have begun to develop and you've probably started wearing a bra. You may have started menstruating (getting your period).

Along with these physical changes come other new developments. Suddenly dating is on your mind. With these new issues come many new decisions. Some of these decisions, such as whether or when to have sex and what kind of birth control to use, can change your life. These are serious considerations, and you should know the most you can about your body before you make any big decisions that concern your body.

As you navigate through these changes, there are many people who can help. You might talk to

a parent or a friend. Or you might sort through feelings with a school counselor. When it comes to health issues, one person who can help is a gynecologist. A gynecologist is a doctor who has special training in women's sexual and reproductive health, including breast care, menstrual health, and birth control.

If you have painful periods or other pain in your reproductive organs, a gynecologist can treat these problems. A gynecologist is a knowledgeable source for understanding your body and your reproductive health. He or she can be a neutral resource for any questions you may have that you don't feel comfortable asking your parents or another adult.

But going to the gynecologist may seem scary or embarrassing, since the gynecologist looks at parts you usually keep covered. She may ask questions about sex, about which you may still feel uncertain.

You probably also have many questions: Will you have to take off your clothes? What happens during the exam? Will it hurt?

Going to a gynecologist doesn't have to be scary—when you know the facts. Knowing the facts can help you make smart choices about your sexual and reproductive health. This is part of becoming responsible for your own health and well-being, and becoming a woman.

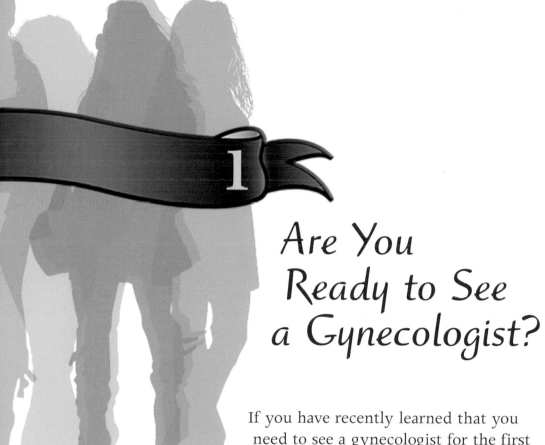

Are You Ready to See a Gynecologist?

If you have recently learned that you need to see a gynecologist for the first time, you probably have many questions. Why is a gynecologist necessary? How should you go about finding one? Do you have to tell your parents? Here is some basic information you should know before scheduling your appointment.

Why Not Just Go to a Regular Doctor?

A gynecologist is a doctor who takes care of women. He or she has special training in women's sexual and reproductive health, including breast care, menstrual health, birth control and pregnancy, and sexually transmitted diseases (STDs). Gynecologists are also trained in obstetrics, the care of pregnant women and childbirth. That's why they are called obstetrician-gynecologists,

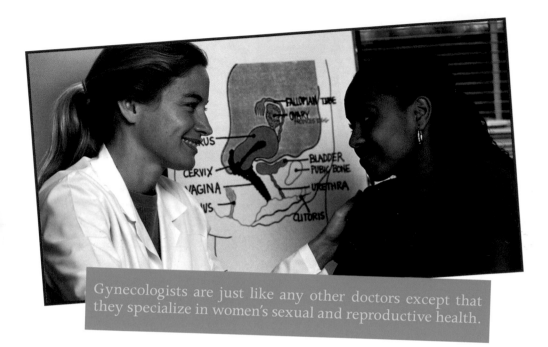

Gynecologists are just like any other doctors except that they specialize in women's sexual and reproductive health.

or OB/GYNs. If you become pregnant, your OB/GYN can provide proper care so that you give birth to a healthy baby. In fact, an OB/GYN will probably help you deliver your baby.

Making the Right Choice

Because gynecologists are specialists who have had extra training in gynecology, an OB/GYN is the best choice for assistance with health problems associated with menstruation and female reproductive organs. Although you can still go to your family doctor for other health matters, gynecologist visits are an important part of growing up and taking care of yourself.

When Should You Start Going to a Gynecologist?

Traditionally, doctors have advised women to have their first gynecological checkup when they become sexually active or have reached the age of eighteen (whichever comes first). Gynecologists now recommend that girls start going anywhere from thirteen to fifteen years old. You may want to visit a gynecologist to talk about periods, birth control, and sexually transmitted diseases. After your first visit, you should have an exam annually or as advised by your health-care provider.

There are many reasons why you might need to see a gynecologist. If you are experiencing irregular or unusually heavy periods or if you think you may have a vaginal infection (which may not be sexually transmitted), it's a good idea to make an appointment, no matter what your age. Other reasons you might want to see a gynecologist include the following:

- If you experience pain during your period or during sexual activity
- If you haven't gotten your period, and you are nearing age seventeen
- If you experience symptoms of STDs or other gynecological disorders
- Before you become sexually active

Choosing a gynecologist is not an easy task. Ask a friend or relative for a referral to a doctor you can feel comfortable around and trust.

Finding a Gynecologist

In general, the best way to find a good doctor is by asking people you know for the names of their doctors. This is called asking for a referral. Many teens use their mother's OB/GYN, or ask her to recommend someone. If you don't feel comfortable discussing this with your mother, ask a friend, a relative, your family doctor, or the school nurse for referrals.

You can also call your local Planned Parenthood clinic. Many hospitals and women's organizations also have referral hotlines. Some health organizations also have clinics where you can pay on a sliding scale, depending on your income.

When choosing a gynecologist, gender may be important to you. You should go with whomever you feel most at ease with.

Something to remember: If your medical insurance is part of an HMO (health maintenance organization), you will probably have to use one of the doctors in its directory. For a list of doctors, call the customer service number at your HMO. Then ask friends and relatives if they're familiar with any of the doctors listed.

What Should You Look For in a Gynecologist?

When choosing a doctor, there are a few qualities you should consider. First, make sure the doctor has been board-certified by the American Board of Obstetrics and Gynecology. This means that, after graduating from medical school and completing a four-year residency (special training course) in obstetrics and gynecology, the doctor has treated women's health conditions for at least two years and has passed an oral exam and a written test showing that he or she has the knowledge and skills to treat women. There are other types of health-care workers who are certified to give annual gynecological checkups. They include nurse practitioners (NP), certified nurse midwives (CMN), and physician's assistants (PA).

It is very important that you feel comfortable with your doctor. You may not know whether or not you do until after your first appointment, but if you don't feel comfortable, don't hesitate to look for another doctor for your next checkup.

Choosing a Man or Woman

In the past, most gynecologists, like most doctors, were men. But now, more and more women are becoming gynecologists. Whether you choose a male or female doctor is up to you. Some women feel more comfortable with a female doctor. Other women do not care or prefer to see a male doctor. Whichever you choose, be assured that all gynecologists—both women and men—are trained to be professional with their patients.

Do I Need to Tell a Parent?

Many teens worry about telling their parent or guardian, since even a routine gynecology checkup can raise sensitive issues about sexuality. It's normal for teens to feel uncomfortable when talking about sex with their parents. But it is always a good idea to keep the lines of communication open. If that seems impossible in your situation, try to find a trusted adult

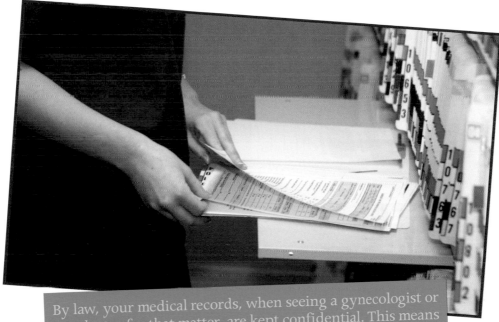

By law, your medical records, when seeing a gynecologist or any doctor for that matter, are kept confidential. This means that no one but you and your doctor has access to them.

you can talk to—an older friend, relative, guidance counselor, or member of the clergy. Talking about it will give you the reassurance you need.

Whether or not you choose to tell your parents, you can still make sure that your doctor visit is confidential. At Planned Parenthood clinics, for instance, you can get a complete gynecological checkup without a parent's permission.

Even a private doctor is required by law to keep your records confidential. That means that if you choose not to let your mother know what went on at your checkup, she'll never find out. If you are sexually active and are going to the gynecologist to find out about birth control options, keep in mind that a diaphragm fitting or birth control pill prescription may turn up on a doctor's bill. So if your parents pay the bill (a likely scenario for most teens), talk to your gynecologist about what to do.

Making the Appointment

When you call the doctor's office to set up an appointment, the receptionist may need to know certain information: your name, age, address, phone number, type of medical insurance, and the reason for your visit. Don't hesitate to tell her if you want to get birth control or if you've been experiencing certain symptoms. Figure out in advance when you might be getting your period so that you can avoid scheduling an appointment at that time. Of course, if you are experiencing painful symptoms, make an appointment as soon as possible.

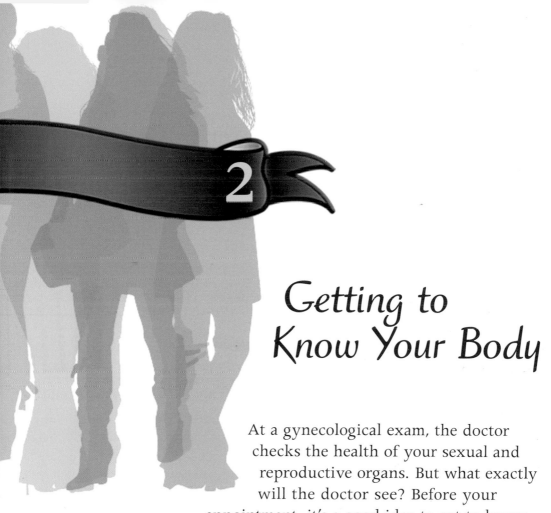

Getting to Know Your Body

At a gynecological exam, the doctor checks the health of your sexual and reproductive organs. But what exactly will the doctor see? Before your appointment, it's a good idea to get to know your own body. What do women's reproductive and sexual organs look like? How do they work together?

By becoming familiar with your sex organs, you'll not only be ready for your appointment, but you can also make good choices about both your health and your sexual behavior.

The Reproductive System

A woman's reproductive system is made up of many organs: the uterus, ovaries, and fallopian tubes; the vulva, clitoris, urethra, and vagina; and the breasts. Each plays a different part in reproduction.

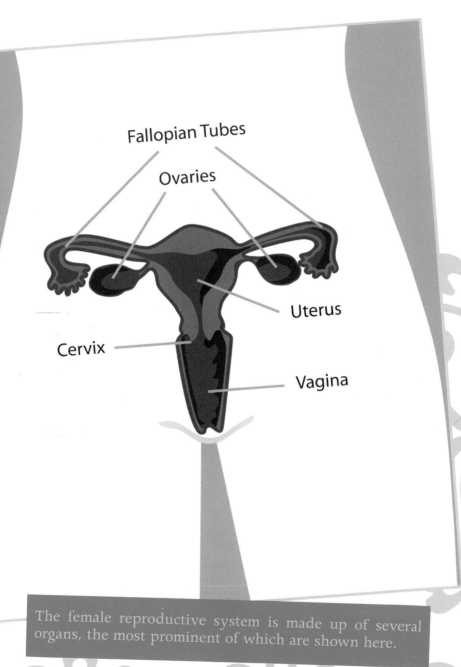

Fallopian Tubes

Ovaries

Uterus

Cervix

Vagina

The female reproductive system is made up of several organs, the most prominent of which are shown here.

The Vulva

A woman's outer genital area, called the vulva, is a soft, fleshy area covered with pubic hair. Between the legs, the vulva is divided into two sets of labia (vaginal lips)—the outer lips (labia majora) and the inner lips (labia minora). Both are soft and sensitive to the touch. These lips partly cover three other areas of the vulva: the clitoris, the urethra (urinary opening), and the vagina.

The Clitoris

The clitoris is the only organ in a woman's body whose single purpose is sexual sensation. The tip (glans) of the clitoris is found toward the top of the vulva. It looks like a tiny knob covered by a hood. This is the most sensitive spot in the entire genital area, and when touched, it can lead to an orgasm, a series of pleasurable sensations. The tip of the clitoris is connected to a network of muscles, veins, nerves, and tissue inside the pubic area that contribute to sexual arousal.

The Urethra

Right below the clitoris is the urinary opening. It looks like a small dot or slit. This is the outer opening of the urethra, a short, thin tube that leads to the bladder. The urethra is about one and a half inches (3.8 centimeters) in length.

10 Facts About Seeing the Gynecologist

1. Traditionally, doctors have advised women to have their first gynecological checkup when they become sexually active or have reached the age of eighteen (whichever comes first).

2. Doctors are required by law to keep your medical files confidential, unless it's about a life-threatening situation.
3. The menstrual cycle (from the Latin word *mensis*, or "month") is the monthly cycle during which the reproductive organs prepare for the possibility of impregnation.
4. One of the first things the doctor does is obtain a history of your health.
5. If you plan to have your visit paid for by your insurance, you should take along your insurance identification card so you can be billed properly.
6. Most of the time, the physical exam has three parts: a check of your general health (weight, blood pressure, heartbeat), the breast exam, and the pelvic exam.
7. PMS is the name for a group of physical and emotional changes that some women go through before their menstrual period begins.
8. One thing your doctor will need to know is whether you are sexually active, and if so, at what age you began having sex.
9. In the past, most gynecologists, like most doctors, were men. But now, more and more women are becoming gynecologists.
10. At Planned Parenthood clinics, for instance, you can get a complete gynecological checkup without a parent's permission.

The Vagina and Cervix

The vagina (or vaginal canal) is the opening to a woman's inner reproductive organs. When a woman has sexual intercourse, this is where the man's penis enters. During childbirth, a baby emerges. Inside the vagina are soft, sensitive folds of skin. The vaginal walls are lubricated with a natural fluid.

The innermost part of the vagina is called the cervix. The cervix is the base of the uterus (womb). It is a pliable, nose-shaped canal with a small dimple. The dimple is the opening into the uterus. When a woman gives birth, the cervix softens and expands enormously for the baby to come out.

The Uterus, Ovaries, and Fallopian Tubes

At the top of the vaginal canal, just below your bladder, are the reproductive organs: the uterus, ovaries, and fallopian tubes. These are the organs that work together to get an egg ready for conception.

The uterus, or womb, is a powerful muscle that holds the growing fetus when a woman is pregnant. When a woman is not pregnant, it is only about as big as a closed fist.

On both sides of the uterus are the two ovaries. They are about the size and shape of unshelled almonds. The ovaries have two functions: They produce eggs (ova) and female sex hormones, including estrogen and progesterone.

At the top of the uterus, extending from both sides like ram's horns, are the two fallopian tubes. Sometimes called oviducts (literally, "egg tubes"), they are the tubes through which the egg travels each month from ovary to uterus. They are about 4 inches (10 cm) long. Inside are microscopic hairs (cilia) that propel the egg toward the uterus. The cilia are in constant motion. When sperm are inside, they also move the sperm toward the egg.

The Menstrual Cycle

The menstrual cycle (from the Latin word *mensis*, or "month") is the monthly cycle during which the reproductive organs prepare for the possibility of impregnation. When pregnancy doesn't happen, the body rids itself of the extra blood and nutrients that have gathered in the uterus to nourish a growing baby (fetus). This is the menstrual flow, or period. In most women, the cycle takes about twenty-eight days.

Ovulation: The Egg's Journey Begins

Each month, in response to messages sent by hormones, one egg comes out of the ovary. This is called ovulation. (You probably won't notice ovulation, but you may feel a twinge or cramp in your lower stomach or back at this time.) After ovulation, the egg is swept into the funnel-shaped end of one of the fallopian tubes (oviducts) and begins its journey to the uterus, moved along by wavelike contractions of the tube.

If a man's sperm meets the egg while it is in the outer third of the fallopian tube (nearest the ovaries), the egg will be fertilized. Also called conception, this means a woman has become pregnant. It is most likely to occur within one day of ovulation, but it can happen any time the egg is in the oviduct.

If the egg is fertilized, it will continue traveling toward the uterus, a process that takes five or six days. Then it will attach itself to the wall of the uterus and begin to grow and develop. In about nine months, a baby will be ready to be born.

If the egg is not fertilized, it flows out of the vagina during the menstrual period.

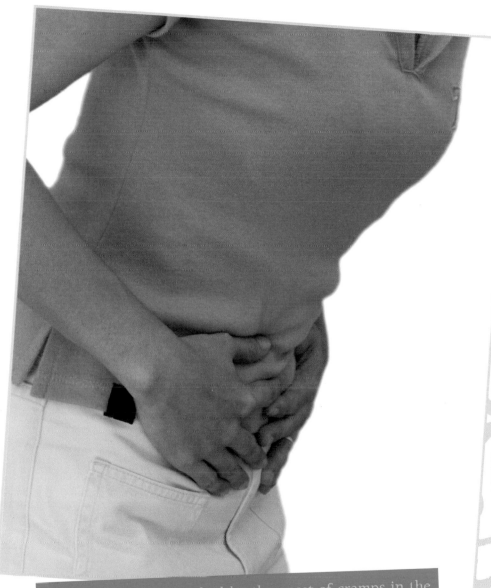

Ovulation is often marked by the onset of cramps in the lower abdomen or back. This and other symptoms are called premenstrual syndrome, or PMS.

Menstruation

At the same time as the egg is making its way down the fallopian tube, the uterus is preparing for the embryo that might soon be developing. Its preparations are governed by hormones, especially estrogen and progesterone.

Just before ovulation, estrogen is released by the maturing egg. Estrogen increases the blood supply to the uterus and causes the uterine lining (endometrium) to grow and thicken in preparation for a potential embryo (a developing fetus). After the egg is released from the ovary, progesterone causes the endometrium to begin secreting substances to nourish the embryo. If the egg has been fertilized, it will begin to grow into an embryo once it reaches the uterus.

If the egg has not been fertilized, the ovary produces less and less estrogen and progesterone. As hormone levels drop, most of the uterine lining is shed. This is menstruation.

The bottom layer of the uterine lining remains to form a new lining. Then a new egg starts growing and secreting estrogen, a new uterine lining grows, and the cycle begins again.

The Gynecological Exam

You may be nervous about your first visit to the gynecologist. Will the doctor ask you embarrassing questions? Will the examination hurt? Will you have to undress completely?

If the thought of getting a checkup makes you nervous, you are not alone. But chances are, you'll find out it isn't as bad as you feared.

Before the Exam

Before starting the exam, the doctor will probably want to meet with you in his or her office or in the examining room to find out a bit about your background and your concerns. If you want to, you can ask a parent or a friend to come in with you for this discussion. But if you want to talk to the doctor about something confidential, ask your parent to wait outside.

Visits to the gynecologist usually start out with your doctor asking you various questions about your health for use in the examination.

You may want to write down any questions you have about your body or your health before your appointment. If you've scheduled your visit because of a specific problem, write down your symptoms, when they began, and whether they've gotten better or worse over time. If there is something you want to talk about, feel free to bring it up.

Don't worry if you forget to ask something, though. You can always call back after the appointment and talk to the doctor or a nurse over the phone.

Health History

One of the first things the doctor does is obtain a history of your health. You might be asked to fill out a form with this information. Once you have filled out the form, the doctor will talk to you about your answers.

The doctor may ask how old you were when you got your first period, the date your most recent period started and whether it is regular, whether you are sexually active or are planning to be, whether you take birth control pills or other medications, and whether you are or ever have been pregnant. You will also be asked about any illnesses you've had and about your family health history.

It's a good idea to check with a parent or family member before your appointment to get this information. Or you could refer your gynecologist to your family doctor, who probably has this information in his or her files.

In addition to looking at your medical history, the doctor may ask about your health habits. If you smoke, use drugs or alcohol, or eat a high-fat diet, you should discuss this with your doctor. These habits not only have a bad effect on your overall health, but they can increase your risk of certain gynecological disorders. Also, if you smoke or take drugs while you are pregnant, you can harm your baby.

If you plan to have your visit paid for by your insurance, one other piece of information you should take along is your insurance identification card so you can be billed properly. Be ready to give your card to the receptionist, either before or after your appointment.

Talking to Your Doctor: Honesty Counts

One thing your doctor will need to know is whether you are sexually active, and if so, at what age you began having sex and other matters that you would not normally tell a stranger. You might feel squeamish about revealing these personal details. But remember, knowing about your sex life is part of a gynecologist's job. Without this information, the doctor would not be able to give you the best advice and care for your reproductive health. Your answers should be honest and open.

What you tell your doctor should be kept confidential—no one else should know (not even your parents)—but before you go in for an exam, you should make sure that your doctor adheres to confidentiality policies. Doctors are required by law to keep your medical files confidential, unless it's about a life-threatening situation. Only by being honest will you be able to get the complete health care you need.

In the Examining Room

Most of the time, the physical exam has three parts: a check of your general health (weight, blood pressure, heartbeat), the breast exam, and the pelvic exam. After that, the doctor may perform some extra blood tests or cultures for sexually transmitted diseases or anemia. The actual checkup usually takes no more than twenty minutes, though of course you will probably be at the clinic longer filling out paperwork and answering general questions.

Sometimes, especially with teens on a first visit, a doctor might only want to talk to you or do a general exam, not a pelvic or breast exam. If this is your first time seeing a gynecologist,

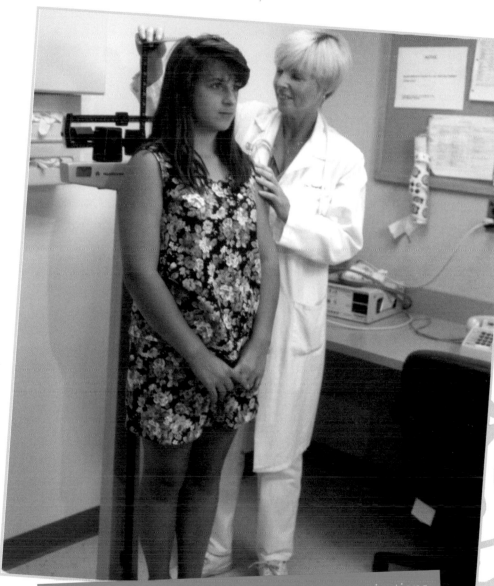

Your gynecologist will perform routine examinations, such as checking your height and weight, to determine your general overall health.

say so. Ask the doctor to go slowly and explain what he or she is doing. If at any time during the exam you feel uncomfortable, speak up.

Before the exam, the doctor may ask you for a urine sample, but even if she or he doesn't, it's a good idea to use the bathroom first, since a full bladder could interfere with the pelvic exam. Most of the time, you won't need to get fully unclothed, but some doctors prefer if you get into an examining gown. (If so, the opening usually goes in front.) This might feel uncomfortable, but remember that seeing undressed women is just part of the doctor's job.

Breast Exam

The purpose of the breast exam is to make sure that your breasts are healthy. Because breast cancer is extremely rare in women younger than twenty-five, it is unlikely that any lump that is found would be cancer. However, there are some types of cysts (enlarged glands) and lumps (called fibroadenomas) found in young women that, though usually harmless, should be watched.

During the breast exam, the doctor will ask you to lie back on a table. He or she will look at your breasts to check their appearance. Then the gynecologist will check for unusual lumps by touching your breasts. If your breasts are tender (this is common when breasts are growing and just before your period), it is usual to feel a bit of discomfort during this exam. But if anything hurts, don't be afraid to speak up.

It's a good idea to do a breast self-exam at home every month. If you are not sure how to do this, ask the doctor or nurse to teach you.

MYTHS & FACTS

MYTH If you are not sexually active, there is no reason to see a gynecologist.

FACT Traditionally, doctors have advised women to have their first gynecological checkup when they become sexually active or have reached the age of eighteen (whichever comes first). It is now recommended that you see a gynecologist as young as thirteen to learn about sexual health. There are many reasons why you might need to see a gynecologist. If you are experiencing irregular or unusually heavy periods, if you are worried because you have never gotten your period, or if you think you may have a vaginal infection (which may not be sexually transmitted), it's a good idea to make an appointment, no matter what your age.

MYTH You will feel more comfortable with a female doctor than with a male doctor.

FACT Whether you choose a male or female doctor is up to you. Some women feel more comfortable with a female doctor. Other women do not care or prefer to see a male doctor. Whichever you choose, be assured that all gynecologists—both women and men—are trained to be very professional with their patients.

MYTHS &

MYTH If you tell the gynecologist that you had sex or asked about birth control, he or she will tell your parents.

FACT Don't worry. Anything you tell your doctor will be kept confidential—no one else will know (not even your parents). In fact, doctors are required by law to keep your medical files confidential, unless it's about a life-threatening situation. If you are concerned about privacy, talk to your gynecologist. He or she can reassure you and tell you what the office's policies are.

MYTH A pelvic exam is painful.

FACT Although a pelvic exam can be slightly uncom-fortable and you may feel some pressure, the exam should not be painful.

MYTH It's embarrassing to be examined by a gynecologist.

FACT Everyone feels a little apprehensive about her first visit to a gynecologist. However, your doctor will do his or her best to make you feel comfortable during the exam. Remember that seeing undressed women is just part of the doctor's job, and your health is the main issue. Feel free to voice any concerns or feelings of embarrassment. You are not the first person to feel that way, and your doctor will understand.

The Pelvic Exam

After checking your breasts, the doctor does an exam of your pelvic organs. For this part of the exam, you will need to slide your feet into footrests (called stirrups) and lie on the table with your legs raised and knees spread apart. It's normal to feel uncomfortably exposed in this position. To put you at ease, the doctor may cover your lower body with a sheet. (Feel free to request a sheet if he or she doesn't offer one.)

As with the breast exam, the doctor will look first and then touch. First he or she looks at the outer genital area (vulva) and the opening to your vagina, making sure that everything looks fine. Then, to get a better view of the inside of the vagina and the cervix, he or she gently inserts a slender instrument called a speculum into the vagina.

The speculum is a tube-shaped instrument made of metal or plastic. Once inside, it opens slightly and holds the vaginal walls apart. (This shouldn't hurt, although you might feel some pressure. Try relaxing your muscles as much as possible, and if this doesn't help, tell the doctor. He or she can readjust the speculum or try a smaller size.)

The speculum lets the doctor see all the way to your cervix. He or she will examine the walls of the vagina and check your cervix for anything unusual. Some doctors keep a hand mirror nearby and will let you look at your cervix. This is a good opportunity to learn more about your body.

During the short time the speculum is in place, the doctor may also take a sample of cells from the cervix to test for abnormal cell growth. This is called a Pap smear. If you have symptoms of, are at risk for, or request testing for an infection or STD, the

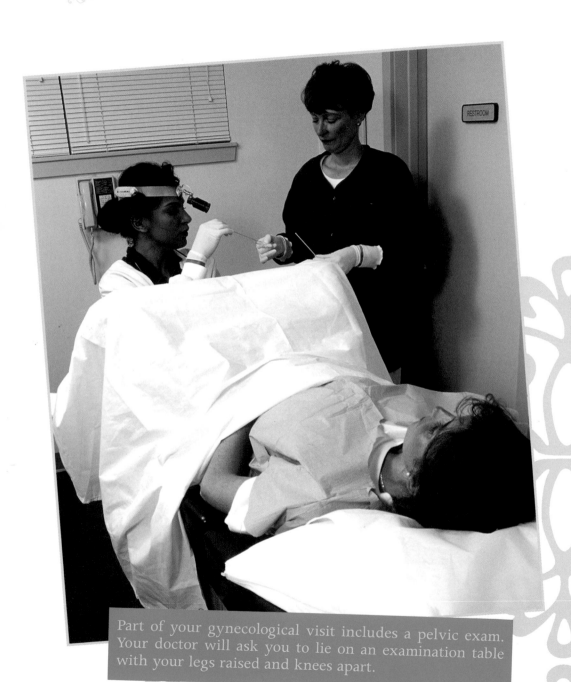

Part of your gynecological visit includes a pelvic exam. Your doctor will ask you to lie on an examination table with your legs raised and knees apart.

doctor may also take a culture for gonorrhea and chlamydia, another culture to check for yeast infection or bacterial vaginitis, and a bit of vaginal discharge to examine for infection. This should not hurt, although you may have some spotting for a day or two after the test. (Spotting is more likely if you are pregnant or if you have a vaginal infection.) The cells are swabbed onto a slide and sent to a laboratory, where a trained technician will examine them. Results from the tests are usually back within one to two weeks. If you feel nervous about getting a call at your home, you might want to ask how your doctor contacts his or her patients. If you wish, you can request that the results be mailed to you.

At some point during the exam, the doctor will put on a clean plastic glove and insert one or two gloved fingers into the vagina. He or she will reach up to the cervix, while the other hand gently presses on your stomach from the outside. By doing this, your doctor can feel the uterus, ovaries, and fallopian tubes. This test is done to check their size, position, and shape. The doctor can also locate any unusual growths, swelling, tenderness, or pain. You should feel some pressure, but not pain. If you do feel pain, let the doctor know.

Other Tests

Besides the Pap test and breast exam, there are a few other tests you can have done by an OB/GYN. Which ones you receive depends on your age and whether you are at risk for any disease. Tests for teens include:

• Blood count, a test for detecting anemia (low iron) or other infections.

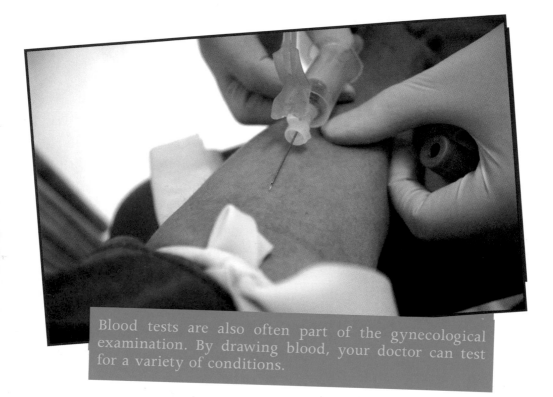

Blood tests are also often part of the gynecological examination. By drawing blood, your doctor can test for a variety of conditions.

- Urinalysis, a test done on urine to look for changes that might be a sign of illness, especially urinary tract or bladder infection.
- Cholesterol test, a blood test done every five years to check levels of cholesterol, a substance that helps carry fat through the blood.
- Mammogram, an X-ray of the breasts to detect breast cancer. This is generally done only when you are in your thirties or forties, but it may be done earlier if you have an unusual lump in your breast.
- Sexually transmitted diseases tests.
- Human immunodeficiency virus (HIV) blood test to determine whether you have acquired the virus that can cause acquired immunodeficiency syndrome (AIDS).

4

Your Reproductive Health

You may have questions about sex and birth control. You may also have other questions about your reproductive health in general (and what measures to take to maintain your reproductive health throughout your life). By going to the gynecologist, you have a good opportunity to find out about all of these things in one sitting. Even if you're not yet sexually active, you can benefit from learning about birth control. That way, you'll have the facts when it's time to decide what's right for you. Some methods are available only from a doctor or health-care provider.

Chances are, your first gynecology checkup will be what doctors call a "well woman exam"—a routine checkup to confirm that you are healthy. But sometimes a missed period, serious cramps, or other symptoms can raise your concerns enough to visit the gynecologist.

Premenstrual syndrome is an uncomfortable experience for many women. Physical and emotional changes may make you feel sick.

Premenstrual Syndrome (PMS)

PMS is the name for a group of physical and emotional changes that some women go through before their menstrual period begins. The symptoms follow a pattern. They reappear at about the same time each month and go away after your period has begun.

Physical changes include breast tenderness or swelling, bloating, weight gain, headache, fatigue, constipation, and clumsiness. Emotional changes include depression, irritability, anxiety, tension, mood swings, inability to concentrate, and change in sex drive. You don't need to have all of these to have PMS, and

Chocolate and beverages with caffeine may satisfy a craving, but consuming them during PMS may make you wish you hadn't done so.

the severity of symptoms can vary from month to month.

So far, doctors do not know what causes PMS or why some women are affected more than others. Researchers are investigating whether estrogen and progesterone (the hormones that stimulate menstruation) may act with chemicals in the brain to cause some PMS symptoms.

There is no cure for PMS, but there are ways to cope. To prevent swelling, bloating, or breast tenderness, steer clear of salt and caffeine for two weeks before your period. Reducing caffeine (found in coffee, tea, colas, and chocolate) can also calm anxiety, insomnia, and irritability. If you feel depressed, talk to a close friend, family member, or counselor. Schedule time for energizing exercise, and make sure you get extra sleep.

When Your Period Doesn't Go Away

Cycles that vary widely in length are common in teenagers. But if your cycle continues to be irregular more than a year after you begin menstruating, it's a good idea to get a checkup.

10 Questions to Ask Your Gynecologist

1 What do you test for in a routine exam?

2 Is what I say during the exam confidential?

3 Can a friend be with me during the exam?

4 When will I get the test results? How will I get them?

5 Can you help me figure out the best birth control option for me?

6 Do I have a risk for anemia? If so, would you recommend iron supplements?

7 Should I be doing breast self-exams? If so, can you show me how to do them?

8 What over-the-counter medication, if any, would you recommend for cramps?

9 What can I do myself to alleviate PMS symptoms?

10 Can I call you, or is there someone in your office whom I can call, if I have any further questions?

When your period doesn't go away, it may be time to see a gynecologist. There are many reasons why this may happen. Instead of worrying, you should have it checked out.

Usually this is due to changes in the balance of the hormones estrogen and progesterone. Bleeding for more than one week may also be caused by a uterine fibroid.

What you should do is see your doctor. A thorough pelvic exam will determine if you have a fibroid. If not, birth control pills should put your cycle back on track.

When Your Period Is Unusually Heavy or Light

It is normal for menstrual flow to vary by day or month, especially in teenagers who are just beginning to menstruate. Bleeding or spotting between periods is also common and not usually cause for alarm. But prolonged, heavy, or irregular bleeding can also indicate more serious conditions, so see your doctor.

If you do not ovulate regularly (common in teens whose cycles are just getting established), your body can experience a buildup of estrogen, which leads to late periods and very heavy bleeding. Other causes of abnormally heavy periods include pregnancy or miscarriage, STDs, cervical problems, or vaginitis. Taking amphetamines or over-the-counter diet aids can also increase menstrual flow and cramping.

If you have light, irregular bleeding, your doctor may suggest waiting a month or two to see if your system rights itself. You may be able to stabilize your menstrual flow by reducing stress and changing your diet. For heavy bleeding, your doctor might prescribe estrogen pills. And ask about iron pills to offset anemia (low iron) from blood loss.

Urinary Tract and Bladder Infections

A urinary tract infection (UTI), which is very common, is an infection of the urinary tract. The infection can happen in the urethra or the bladder. (More serious infections occasionally spread to the kidneys.) About one in five women will have at least one urinary tract infection at some point in her life. Many women have more than one. Fortunately most UTIs are not serious. They are easily treatable with antibiotics.

The first sign is a sudden strong urge to urinate every few minutes, followed by a sharp pain or burning sensation in the urethra, even though almost no urine comes out. This cycle repeats several times a day or night. You may also have pain or soreness in the lower abdomen, back, or sides.

Urinary tract infections (UTIs) are usually marked by lower abdominal pain. You may also have pain in your back or on your sides.

UTIs are usually caused by bacteria, which travel from the bowel to the urethra and bladder (and occasionally to the kidneys). Women can also get urinary tract infections after sexual intercourse, when bacteria from the vaginal area can be brought into the urethra. STDs, such as trichomoniasis and chlamydia, can also cause UTIs.

If you have a UTI, you should see your doctor, especially if symptoms continue for forty-eight hours or go away and come back. Call the doctor right away if you also have chills, fever, vomiting, or pain in the kidneys (which may mean the infection has spread to the kidneys, a serious problem that requires immediate medical treatment); if there is blood or pus in your urine; or if you are pregnant, have diabetes, or had kidney or urinary tract infections when you were a child.

Now that you know the facts, going to the gynecologist may seem a lot easier than you thought. It's a good idea to keep learning as much as you can, even after that first appointment is over. Remember, going to the gynecologist is an important part of becoming responsible for your own health and well-being.

Glossary

clitoris The organ in a woman's body that gives sexual pleasure.

fallopian tube The tube connecting an ovary to the uterus.

gynecologist A doctor who specializes in women's reproductive health.

health maintenance organization (HMO) An organization that provides medical insurance.

mammogram An X-ray of the breasts to detect abnormalities including cancer.

menstruation The shedding of the uterine lining, occurring in women approximately every twenty-eight days.

OB/GYN An obstetrician/gynecologist; a doctor who specializes in women's reproductive health.

obstetrics The care of pregnant women.

ovarian cyst A fluid-filled sac that develops when a follicle in the ovary fails to rupture and release an egg.

ovary The gland that produces the female sex hormones estrogen and progesterone.

ovulation The release of an egg by the ovary.

Pap test A test run on cells taken from the cervix, checking for abnormalities.

pelvic inflammatory disease A general term referring to infection and inflammation of a woman's internal reproductive organs.

pregnancy Carrying a developing fetus within the body.

premenstrual syndrome A set of physical and emotional symptoms, such as bloating and irritability, that occur in a woman prior to the menstrual period.

sexually transmitted disease A disease spread through sexual intercourse.

speculum A tube-shaped instrument that holds the vaginal walls open during a gynecological exam.

urinary tract infection A bacterial infection causing inflammation of the urethra, kidneys, and bladder.

uterine fibroid A benign tumor that grows inside or outside the uterus.

uterus The muscular organ inside of which a fetus grows.

vagina The opening to a woman's inner reproductive organs.

vaginitis An infection of the vaginal walls and vulva.

vulva A woman's outer genital area.

For More Information

CDC National STD Hotline
(800) 227-8922
Spanish: (800) 344-7432

This twenty-four-hour hotline offers confidential information on sexually transmitted diseases.

Center for Young Women's Health
Children's Hospital Boston
333 Longwood Avenue, 5th Floor
Boston, MA 02115
(617) 355-2994
Web site: http://www.youngwomenshealth.org

This center's Web site offers information on various health topics as well as information on gynecological exams and what to expect.

Web Sites

Due to the changing nature of Internet links, Rosen Publishing has developed an online list of Web sites related to the subject of this book. This site is updated regularly. Please use this link to access the list:

http://www.rosenlinks.com/gh/gyne

For Further Reading

Bell, Ruth. *Changing Bodies, Changing Lives: A Book for Teens on Sex and Relationships*. 3rd ed. New York, NY: Three Rivers Press, 1998.

Boston Women's Health Book Collective. *Our Bodies, Ourselves: A New Edition for a New Era*. New York, NY: Touchstone, 2005.

Devillers, Julia. *GirlWise: How to Be Confident, Capable, Cool, and in Control*. New York, NY: Three Rivers Press, 2002.

Fingerson, Laura. *Girls in Power: Gender, Body, and Menstruation in Adolescence*. Albany, NY: State University of New York Press, 2006.

Girls' Life magazine editors. *The Girls' Life Guide to Growing Up*. Hillsboro, OR: Beyond Words Publishing, 2000.

Stanley, Deborah. *Sexual Health Information for Teens: Health Tips About Sexual Development, Human Reproduction, and Sexually Transmitted Diseases* (Teen Health Series). Detroit, MI: Omnigraphics, 2003.

Bibliography

Boston Women's Health Book Collective. *Our Bodies, Ourselves: A New Edition for a New Era*. New York, NY: Touchstone, 2005.

Britannica Online. "Human Reproductive System." Retrieved August 2006 (http://www.search.eb.com/eb/article-9110811).

Centers for Disease Control and Prevention. "Pelvic Inflammatory Disease–CDC Fact Sheet." Retrieved August 2006 (http://www.cdc.gov/std/PID/STDFact-PID.htm).

Endometriosis Association. "What Is Endometriosis?" Retrieved August 2006 (http://www.endometriosisassn.org/endo.html).

Manassiev, Nikolai, and Malcolm I. Whitehead, eds. *Female Reproductive Health*. Abingdon, UK: Taylor & Francis, 2003.

McCloskey, Jenny. *Your Sexual Health*. San Francisco, CA: Halo Books, 1993.

Planned Parenthood. "GYN Exams." Retrieved August 2006 (http://www.plannedparenthood.org/sexual-health/women-health/gyn-exams.htm).

WebMd. "Sexual Health: Your Guide to the Female Reproductive System." Retrieved August 2006 (http://www.webmd.com/content/article/9/2953_484.htm).

WebMD. "Sexual Health: Your Guide to Premenstrual Syndrome." Retrieved August 2006 (http://www.webmd.com/content/article/10/2953_497.htm).

Index

Photo Credits

Designer: Evelyn Horovicz; **Editor:** Nicholas Croce
Photo Research: Amy Feinberg